GW00771047

MIKIMOTO

© 2008 Assouline Publishing
601 West 26th Street, 18th floor
New York, NY 10001, USA
Tel.: 212 989-6810 Fax: 212 647-0005
www.assouline.com

ISBN: 978 2 7594 0258 8

Printed in China

MIKIMOTO

NICK FOULKES

ASSOULINE

e ven in our secular and scientific age, the pearl retains its mystery. Its luster and allure captivate a broad spectrum of admirers, and it has worked its way into our collective culture, whether through Captain Jack Sparrow and his *Black Pearl* or Vermeer's enigmatic portrait *Girl with the Pearl Earring.*

Yet man's enslavement to the pearl's iridescent beauty also threatened its survival. Mollusks naturally form pearls as a defensive response to irritants such as sand or parasites. Subsequently, the oyster secretes layers of nacre to coat the foreign body, resulting in a pearl. Finding pearls, then, had always been a matter of chance, and the more oysters harvested, the greater the likelihood of discovering pearls. That we continue to enjoy the pearl, that it is still a treasured gift to loved ones, and that it remains the jewel of choice for glamorous women around the world is thanks to one man, Kokichi Mikimoto.

Mikimoto was determined to find a new way of stimulating oysters to produce pearls. This thoughtful man, whose name would one day become synonymous with the finest pearls, was convinced he could change the world of the pearl. Mikimoto devoted his long life to this aim, and it was by cultivating pearls that he preserved the precious tradition of pearl jewelry for women today and for generations to come. He pioneered the process of cultivating pearls, much as if they were grapes in the great vineyards of Bordeaux. Today almost all pearl jewelry is made with pearls reared according to his method.

The pearl is remarkable. Unique among jewels, it is the product of a living organism, not a mined mineral, and the mystery of its creation has ensnared mankind's imagination for millennia. To mystery is added irony; oysters, today a delicacy, were once viewed as little better than junk food. Indeed, the story is that Lord Burlington built the eponymous arcade in London with a roof not to afford shoppers protection against the elements, but to stop them from throwing their empty oyster shells over his walls. For centuries mankind speculated how the humble oyster—the ugly mollusk, food of the masses—could produce an object of such beauty.

Long before the formations of nature were scientifically understood, many of its fruits were explained by the Greeks as being of divine origin. Coral was said to have come about when seaweed was wrapped around Medusa's fearsome head, turning the plant to stone. The story of the pearl was equally picturesque, and involved the goddess Aphrodite—or Venus, as she was known to the Romans. In this myth, as Aphrodite rose from the sea, she shook her long golden hair, and the droplets of water that showered from her tresses fell back into the sea as pearls. Long after the civilizations that had venerated Venus Anadyomene as a goddess had crumbled, the image of the goddess of love rising from the ocean dominated the cultural imagination of the Western world. Often she is seen standing on a shell, most famously of course in Botticelli's depiction.

b y virtue of the pearl's association with Venus, the ancients, perhaps unwittingly, understood much about the pearl, its origin, and its importance as a gift of love. To them, the pearl had divine powers. The natural historian of the Roman Era, Pliny, described them as occupying "the very highest position among all valuables." When the Roman emperor Caligula made his horse a senator, he garlanded the steed with a pearl necklace. Ancient Romans also believed that pearls signified marital bliss. They were the ultimate status symbol, and their use was governed by a law that restricted them to people of rank. Similar sumptuary laws were also invoked in future civilizations to maintain the pearl's exclusivity. Even cultures as diverse as those of China and Babylon attributed life-giving powers to pearls.

During the Dark Ages, the Eastern Roman Empire of Byzantium kept the pearl's importance alive, evoking its divine heritage by using the natural jewel to decorate religious artifacts. The complex satellites of meaning that orbited around this perfectly formed sphere included everything from sex to sanctity, enfolding both pre-Christian and Christian beliefs into one mystical whole, around which stories and symbolism accumulated like the layer upon layer of nacre around the pearl.

In their book *Pearls: Ornament and Obsession*, Kristin Joyce and Shellei Addison explain that early Christians saw the pearl as "an emblem of both Christ and the Virgin Mary and a representation of the soul housed within the earthly body." One of the most intriguing figures of the early Christian world, Saint Margaret of Antioch, was closely associated with pearls. Joyce and Addison note that "before long, Christian pearl imagery became centered in Saint Margaret of Antioch, whose name was derived from *murawa, murwari,* or *mirwareed,* the Persian word for pearl, which translates as 'child of light.' Saint Margaret, in fact, was closely identified with the goddess Aphrodite, a wealthy sacred prostitute, who, in Christian history, converted to the faith and gave all her possessions to the Church. Similarly, the 'pearly gates' that came to symbolize the entrance to the Kingdom of Heaven resembled Aphrodite's own pearly gate—the entrance to her sexual paradise."[1]

With such mystical symbolism, it is not surprising that the consumption of pearls was in some cases literal. Centuries of association with divinity accounted for the medical properties that were ascribed to the pearl, and there were those who seriously believed the pearl was a near-universal panacea. An early remedy for epilepsy involved pearls as a key ingredient in a potion that also included the crushed skull of an evildoer and the hooves of an elk; while one noted Hapsburg physician was fond of prescribing *aqua perlata,* or pearl water, which he recommended as "most excellent for restoring the strength and almost for resuscitating the dead."[2]

But the most famous pearl eater of all was Queen Cleopatra. According to Pliny, the queen enjoyed her pearls dissolved, much as, say, soluble aspirins. "There have been two pearls that were the largest in the whole of history; both were owned by Cleopatra, the last of the Queens of Egypt—they had come down to her through the hands of the Kings of the East," records Pliny in his

Natural History. "In accordance with previous instructions, the servants placed in front of her only a single vessel containing vinegar, the strong, rough quality of which can melt pearls. She was at the moment wearing in her ears those remarkable and truly unique works of nature. Mark Antony was full of curiosity to see what in the world she was going to do. She took one earring off and dropped the pearl in the vinegar, and when it was melted, swallowed it."[3] In another telling of this famous tale, Cleopatra had bet Mark Antony that she could spend 10 million sesterces on a dinner. She subsequently drank the pearl mixture to win the bet.

O f course this was probably more for the dramatic effect of the *grande geste,* and over the centuries this piece of theater was played out on special occasions. For example, when relations between the then-global superpowers Britain and Spain were tense, "a loyal British nobleman withdrew from the pocket of his velvet breeches a pearl worth 15,000 pounds, pulverized it, dropped it in a glass of wine, and drank a toast to Queen Elizabeth of England and King Philip of Spain. The motive behind this extravagant gesture was to convey to the ambassador of Spain, who was present, that Elizabeth did not need to accept Philip's proposal of marriage and to impress him with the solidity of England's economy. The Spaniard was impressed, even though his own sovereign owned a half-million-dollar pearl as large as a pigeon's egg."[4]

British royals of the sixteenth and seventeenth century were far from the only rulers to be entranced by the pearl. Chinese emperors of millennia long past, the queens of ancient Persia, and the families of the maharajahs of pre-Mogul India all coveted its sensuality and luster. By the latter half of the nineteenth century, the mania for pearls among royal families had reached a zenith. The Hapsburgs, whose imperial dynasty ruled Middle Europe, were famed for their collection. The ballrooms and banquet halls of St. Petersburg's Winter Palace glowed with the suffused luster of Romanov grand duchesses garlanded with rope after rope of pearls, with yet more of the nacreous gems shimmering in the tiaras that were de rigueur on state occasions in czarist Russia. Elsewhere, the Bonaparte dynasty had once more taken control of France, where Napoleon III presided over a luxury-obsessed society with his fashion-mad consort Empress Eugenie, who is credited with introducing the vogue for black and colored pearls in Europe.

●

In England the sybaritic Prince of Wales appeared to have eased his guilty conscience by decking out his wife, the former Princess Alexandra of Denmark, with so many strands of pearls that in some photographs she resembled a Christmas tree. Even that ultimate nineteenth-century royal, Victoria of England, the woman who lent her name to an era of history and occupied her throne for more than sixty years, was not immune to the allure of the pearl. Despite appearing in sober mourning clothes following the death of her beloved husband, Albert, the queen allowed herself the consolation of pearls around her neck and wrists, their chaste glow contrasting with the black bombazine that was the traditional garb of nineteenth-century widowhood.

There could not have been a greater contrast to the glitter and dazzle, the ceremony and splendor, of nineteenth century court life than the existence of a noodle maker in the coastal town of Toba on Honshu, the largest of Japan's islands. Nor could there have been much worth celebrating in this township of three hundred families—especially in the depths of winter. However, on January 25, 1858, there was celebration in the household of the town's noodle maker as his young wife, not yet out of her teens, gave birth to their first child, a son. They gave him the name Kichimatsu, an elision of the words for "luck" and "pine tree" (which symbolized affluence). As the boy grew, he would sometimes go by the name Kokichi. However, it would be by his family name that he and his life's work would become world famous—Mikimoto.

The family grew, and Kokichi's father worked hard to feed his children; in addition to noodles, he sold charcoal and vegetables. It was perhaps the growing demands of his family that caused him to work harder. Subsequently, when Kokichi was only 11, his father became ill, propelling Kokichi into an early adulthood. He conscientiously shouldered the responsibilities of helping the family by entering the vegetable business and praying regularly for his father's health at the local shrine.

Today Kokichi Mikimoto emerges from history as a quasi-mythical character, a little like William Tell of Switzerland or Dick Whittington, who became mayor of London. Viewed through the lens of history, Kokichi's early life seems rich with portents of future greatness; there is the Good Samaritan story of how he saved the life of a sick traveler that he met on the way back to his village, by foot, from Tokyo. There is also the story of how he outwitted unscrupulous fish merchants when there was a bumper catch of mullet—important work in his small fishing village. Kokichi quickly became a person of consequence in his community. Indeed, it is impossible to understand Kokichi Mikimoto outside the context of the time in which he lived. Born at the very end of the Edo period, during which Japan had been almost totally closed to foreign influence, Kokichi grew up in a rapidly shifting world: Values which had held for generations all but disappeared in a few years. Before his death in 1954, Kokichi would witness the most tumultuous period in Japanese history.

The ships of Commodore Perry had already forced the opening of Japan in the early 1850s, and as a youngster Kokichi saw foreign ships anchored in the sea off Toba. A famous story of his teenage years tells of the young Kokichi rowing out to a British navy vessel to sell his vegetables and winning over the wary European mariners, who had sent other merchants packing, with a bravura display of his remarkable juggling skills—skills that he would still be demonstrating well into his nineties. Ahead of his time, Kokichi already understood opportunity beyond his immediate surroundings and circumstances. He was unafraid to interact outside his culture, and this visionary moment in the life of the young entrepreneur foreshadowed the globalization of the brand Mikimoto years later. However, it was the Meiji restoration of the 1860s—which once more placed an emperor god on the throne while a cabal of ministers ran the country—and the ensuing social changes that set Japan and young Kokichi Mikimoto on the path to the world stage. Legislative change in the form of local government affected Kokichi: In the wake of the fame garnered by his acts of kindness to the roadside stranger, he found himself elected to the town council at the age of 22. A year later, the weakening of the once rigid social barriers that had kept the tiered class system intact for centuries enabled him to take a young bride, Ume, who had been born into the social elite of the samurai class.

Kokichi was clearly ambitious, and it seemed that the climate of change and new ideas would favor a young man who combined charisma and imagination with business acumen and thriftiness. Toba is not far from Japan's most revered religious site, the hallowed Shinto Shrine at Ise. In this sacred location, the story of pearls and the divine are once again entwined. Kokichi had been born near one of the richest pearl-fishing areas of Japan: Ago Bay. The sight of the athletic female divers, naked except for a scrap of cloth around their waists, who plunged into the sea to bring pearls from the seabed entranced the young man. On his trip to Tokyo he had seen the high prices paid for pearls, even seed pearls, which were ground up to use in medicine on the Chinese market. An idea was taking root in his fertile mind.

against the backdrop of an increasingly international and socially emancipated Japan, the ambitious Kokichi saw a greater future for himself beyond the safe but parochial business of town noodle maker and vegetable merchant. The 1880s were a formative decade for Kokichi Mikimoto: He took the decisive step to marry, start a family, and move into a new field of business. In 1881, the year of his marriage to Ume, Kokichi began his involvement in what various biographers have called "marine product" by helping to arrange and judge an exhibition of pearls, mother-of-pearl, and shellfish. A few years later, his father died, making Kokichi head of the family, after which he became known as simply Mikimoto. By the latter half of the 1880s, he was chairman of the Shima Marine Product Improvement Association,[5] and his reputation was one of unswerving dedication to perfection. All around him, Mikimoto saw mis-shaped or underdeveloped pearls being sold, and he was disappointed. As one of his biographers stated, "He never approved of greed that would distort beauty."[6] His reputation as a perfectionist reached the capital and, eventually, the imperial court. It was an illustrious beginning that would one day propel Mikimoto all the way to Paris for the 1937 Paris World Exposition where his unique design, Yaguruma, would be showcased alongside those of Europe's leading talents.

for most men, these achievements would have been sufficient. However, Mikimoto looked further into the future. All around the world, increasing prosperity was leading to ever increasing demand for pearls, especially in the United States, which was displacing Europe as the preeminent industrial and economic power. "If this wanton pearl fishing goes on much longer," Mikimoto observed, "there won't be any oysters left in the sea."[7] He was talking to Narayoshi Yanagi—a dignified and patrician figure in the braided and brass-buttoned uniform of the Japanese navy. In his late fifties, Yanagi was the secretary-general of the Japan Fisheries Association.[8] Mikimoto confided his ambition to this older man: to assist nature by establishing pearl farming—the process of artificially gathering and nucleating an oyster with a foreign object to cause the secretion of nacre, which brings about a pearl. In addition to the revolutionary nature of the idea, there were practical difficulties—local people who depended on fishing for their livelihood. Nevertheless intrigued, and seeing the wisdom of the young man's words, Yanagi agreed to lend official backing to the plan and toured Ago Bay looking for suitable sites; he eventually persuaded the villagers of Shinmei Ura and Ojima to go along with the project, and work began in September 1888. As a perfectionist pearl trader who rejected everything but lustrous spheres, Mikimoto learned that Akoya oysters produced the best pearls. Two centuries later, the company that carries his name is still famed for the quality of its Akoya pearls.

Yanagi became increasingly involved, and in 1890 he invited Mikimoto to Tokyo to exhibit at the Third National Industrial Exposition and meet Kakichi Mitsukuri, a professor at Tokyo University and Japan's foremost marine zoologist. Mikimoto learned about the creation of pearls and discussed methods whereby a particle could be introduced into the mantle, the fleshy part of the oyster. But theory was not the hard part; having studied in Britain and America, Professor Mitsukuri was familiar with a prior failed attempt to assist nature in the raising of pearls. Trial and error was the only way for Mikimoto to achieve his goal: He varied everything from the method of opening the shell so that the oyster would survive, to the nature and size of the nucleus inserted, to the oyster's time and depth underwater. He was also alert to the dangers of unscrupulous pearl divers and natural predators such as octopi.

The work placed a strain on Mikimoto's health, his marriage (his wife was tending the noodle shop and making excuses to creditors), and his reputation. As time passed and the much-vaunted pearls failed to appear, many thought the dynamic and ambitious Mikimoto had gone mad. His fortunes reached their nadir one day in 1892, when Mikimoto looked out across the bay and saw the sea turn red. Red tide, or Harmful Algal Bloom, is an extraordinary natural phenomenon, occuring when certain climatic factors cause a sharp rise in plankton. Their sheer multitude alters the appearance of the water, and it seems reddish. Creatures on the seabed, particularly mollusks, are especially vulnerable to the microorganisms, some of which produce harmful toxins. Like an infestation of locusts, the red tide wiped out 5,000 oysters.

It was almost enough to finish Mikimoto; his business and his honor seemed beyond recovery. However, his loyal wife reminded him that there were still a few oyster beds remaining at Ojima Island, which had perhaps not been affected by the red tide. Although Mikimoto felt that his dream was hopeless and unsalvageable, to humor his wife he accompanied her to the island. The oysters in their bamboo baskets at Ojima had been spared, and together the couple checked their remaining mollusks with diligence, if not enthusiasm. On July 11, 1893, the calloused hands of the dutiful samurai's daughter heaved at the rope attached to one of the baskets of oysters, pulling it up to the water's surface for inspection. It was a routine task, but something caught Ume's eye, a glimmer of moonlight in the fleshy folds of the mollusk's body. A pearl! She pried it free. Although the pearl was only semispherical, her husband was vindicated. He had triumphed against scepticism and natural disaster to assist nature in the creation of the world's first cultured pearl. It was as if the gods, whom the ancients had credited with the creation of the pearl, had rewarded Mikimoto's Herculean efforts. Ume opened more oysters and found four more pearls, all half-speherical.

The year 1896 should have been a triumphant one for Mikimoto. He was granted a patent for the "invention" of the semi-spherical pearl. His hard work had been justified. Business flourished, and Mikimoto decided to base his operation on the island where he found his first pearls, renaming it Pearl Island. Soon forty people were living and working there, family members and diving girls, whose modesty Mikimoto now protected under pale robes. His optimism returned. Not yet 40, he set himself the goal of one million oysters in the water by 1901.[9] And then came the cruelest blow. His beloved wife died at age 32 after an operation. She had given Mikimoto five children and also delivered his first five cultured pearls. Mikimoto reacted to his wife's death by immersing himself totally in his work. Although he would live for almost another sixty years, he did not take another spouse; he was wedded to his business.

t he years around the turn of the century were busy ones for Mikimoto. He opened a store in Tokyo's chic shopping district, Ginza, in 1899—Japan's first pearl boutique. And a few years later, in 1905, he would master the spherical pearl. Mikimoto's reaction to his store's success was to send his brother and brother-in-law to the United States to extend the family business worldwide.

Another shining moment for Mikimoto took place across the Atlantic. Following the coronation of the fashion-forward British monarch Edward VII, the king was presented with Mikimoto pearls that had been set into jewelry by Parisian artisans. With this example in mind, Mikimoto concentrated on developing the skills necessary for his company to create and manufacture jewelry every bit the equal of designs found in the capitals of Europe. He would present the finished products at his eponymous showroom. Designing for royalty boosted Mikimoto's prestige with the increasingly affluent bourgeoisie of early-twentieth-century Japan. Ginza was fast developing as a luxury shopping district rivaling even those of Paris and London; early images show the main street as a broad boulevard thronged with elegant shoppers clad in the latest European fashions. Mikimoto's shop was one of the most fashionable, and although he did not travel a great deal himself, he realized the potential of a worldwide market for his pearls.

ikimoto shops first appeared in the world's major cities, including London and Paris, in the years before the outbreak of the First World War. At this time, Mikimoto started to make exhibition pieces, important items of jewelry that would be displayed in Ginza and then go on tour to be inspected and marveled at by the firm's clients, a custom that continues to this day. These were complemented by increasingly spectacular creations for international exhibitions. Mikimoto's name appeared regularly on lists of medalists in the grand expositions that characterized world trade in the late nineteenth and early twentieth centuries. Among the pieces that have been preserved are a military fan, exhibited in 1907 and 1910, that included 805 pearls in its construction and a mini monument, the five-story pagoda that mixed platinum and intricate shellwork with a staggering 12,760 pearls. The pagoda debuted at Philadelphia's 150-year anniversary of independence exposition in 1926.

In that year, Mikimoto, aged 68, made his first and only visit to America as part of a grand tour that encompassed Europe and the natural pearl fields of the Bay of Bengal and the Persian Gulf. America made a deep and enduring impression on the respected elder of the pearl world. He visited the tomb of George Washington and reported to the founder of American democracy on the state of the pearl industry. He also visited the then-greatest living American, Thomas Edison, who was said to have remarked to Mikimoto: "Diamonds and pearls are the only things my laboratory could not produce."

Mikimoto's fondness for the United States and his approval of its values were eventually expressed in one last masterpiece, finished just before the two great nations became locked in war. Mikimoto created a talking point of the 1939 New York World's Fair with the Liberty Bell, executed to one-third scale with a mother-of-pearl center, decorated with 366 diamonds and a staggering 12,250 pearls, its crack faithfully re-created with black pearls. The bell was said to have been worth a million dollars at the time. It is even said that Mikimoto would have donated this extraordinary coup de théâtre if it would have helped avert the conflict.

When war came, Mikimoto's shops around the world shut, and production more or less ceased. Mikimoto publicly distanced himself from the war, a stance that initially brought unpopularity. At the war's end, Mikimoto was well into his eighties, but he welcomed high-ranking visitors to Pearl Island once again; this time they were American and included Jean MacArthur, the popular and pretty wife of the military governor. He also managed to rebuild his business with astonishing rapidity. By the early 1950s, six million oysters were in their beds, secreting layer after layer of nacre to create more pearls to adorn the throats and earlobes of women all over the world. At the time of his death in 1954, the business had made an astonishing comeback, one that could only have been achieved by a man such as Mikimoto.

After Mikimoto's death, the company continued to adhere to its founder's tradition of excellence, and it continued to grow. Once again, geopolitics had a part to play in this chapter of the history of the brand. Japan's emperor and empress, no longer considered gods but still venerated by the people, visited Pearl Island, but it was the American visitors who fueled its success by purchasing pearl jewelry for their wives and lovers. The occupation of Japan initially kept America in the region, and in the ensuing decades Japan became one of the theaters in the war against communism, first in Korea and then in Vietnam. As America and Japan grew ever closer, a string of Mikimoto pearls became a luxury enjoyed by many American newlyweds, including Marilyn Monroe, who was given a Mikimoto necklace by Joe DiMaggio while on their honeymoon in Japan.

As the country regained its prosperity in the years after the war, elegant Japanese women once more turned to Mikimoto for jewelry of all sorts. Following the farsighted vision of the company's founder, Mikimoto's talented jewelers, gemologists, and goldsmiths worked with the finest, most precious material to create jewelry—sometimes using pearls, sometimes not. In 1907, just two years after Mikimoto had harvested his first truly spherical pearls, he opened a goldwork factory. And as Japan recovered its place in the world, the jewelry of Mikimoto began to be recognized around the globe, confirming Mikimoto as a luxury brand. Society and starlets such as Monroe would now accessorize their New Look clothes with a strand of Mikimoto pearls. Its place as one of the world's premier jewelers was recognized by the close of the 1960s, when Mikimoto won the coveted De Beers Diamonds-International Award.

With international recognition came a network of international shops. By 1975 there was a Mikimoto flagship on Fifth Avenue in New York, and since then Mikimoto stores have become part of the modern luxury retail landscape, with posts everywhere from

Las Vegas to Beijing and, indeed, wherever else beautiful women buy, or are given, the most exquisite pearls and jewels.

The pearl has immortalized the Mikimoto name. Today stores around the world perpetuate its reputation for absolute perfection that the founder promulgated during his long and eventful life. It is no coincidence that Mikimoto decided to burn 720,000 inferior-grade pearls in 1932 in front of the Kobe Chamber of Commerce. His public declaration that "such pearls are fuel" assured buyers that only the finest pearls would appear on the global market. While Mikimoto once said he would like to adorn the necks of all women of the world with pearls, it could only be with pearls of the highest quality. The efforts of Kokichi Mikimoto have preserved pearl jewelry for the pleasure of current and future generations of women; without his persistence, the secret to assisting nature in the cultivation of the precious pearl might never have been discovered. Pearls, like so many of the world's resources, could easily have been exploited to the point of extinction.

however, a piece of pearl jewelry, especially a length of perfectly matched, mirrorlike pearls strung on fine silk and fastened with one of Mikimoto's signature clasps is not something that can be hurried. Each millimeter of a pearl's diameter is composed of many layers of nacre; and women must wait while the oyster patiently does its work. Of all the Akoya pearls harvested in one year, only a small number are deemed worthy of the Mikimoto name. This top percentage will be further divided, by hand, by graders who often boast generations of skill. The graders use four quality categories, and only an infinitesimally small number make the coveted top grade. Once graded, pearls are matched for size and tint, a process that can take years. While the universal grading system for a diamond's color, cut, and clarity is known worldwide and adhered to, the Mikimoto grading scale is the only qualified system that accurately and consistently defines a pearl. Such painstaking care deserves respect. Pearls should be the last thing a woman puts on and the first thing she takes off.

mikimoto has extended its legendary quality to embrace the larger South Sea pearls, and it has worked with top designers from around the world to bring out the beauty of the natural miracle that men call "pearls" in a way that is right and suitable for each woman, whether she favors a classic choker or a dramatic rope; a mixture of black, gray, golden, and white pearls; the unique, mysterious shape of the baroque pearl; the conservatism of silk-strung pearls; or the innovation and boldness of a design that brings pearls together with precious metal and colored gemstones.

Pearls continue to captivate women today as they did when Aphrodite rose from the sea. In 2001, Mikimoto named a collection of pearl jewelry after Princess Grace, one of the most glamorous women of the twentieth century. The following year saw the creation of the official Mikimoto crown, to honor Miss Universe. Nor is actress Keira Knightley's connection with the pearl limited to her on-screen persona in the *Pirates of the Caribbean* franchise; when she graced the cover of *Vanity Fair,* she appeared festooned in Mikimoto pearls . . . and little else. Even the Crillon

Ball in Paris, where the daughters of prominent families make their social debut, has seen the likes of Lauren Bush, Amanda Hearst, and Princess Desiree von Hohenlohe enhance their natural elegance and beauty with Mikimoto jewelry.

With the international style icons pairing both dresses and denim with Mikimoto pearls, it is evident that Mikimoto has revolutionized the classic image of the pearl. Each Mikimoto design is an artistic expression fusing the highest grade pearls with an intriguing modern design.

To enter Mikimoto for the first time is to begin a journey of exploration into the world of the pearl that can last a lifetime: Heavy in the hand and cool to the touch, the pearl almost seems to come to life when worn by an elegant woman. That pearls today are a symbol of elegance and classic chic is a testimony to Mikimoto. Like the black dress or the white shirt, the pearl necklace is an important part of any well-dressed woman's wardrobe and acts as a blank canvas that can be defined by its wearer. Wherever there is fashion, there are pearls.

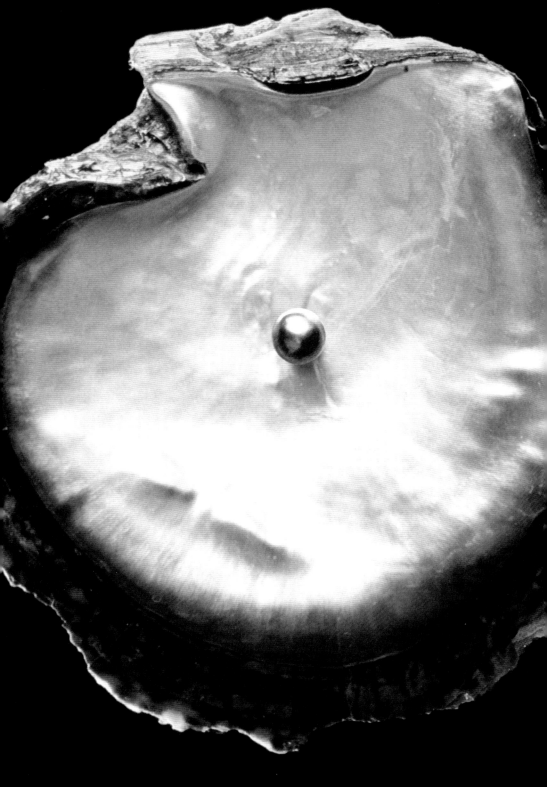

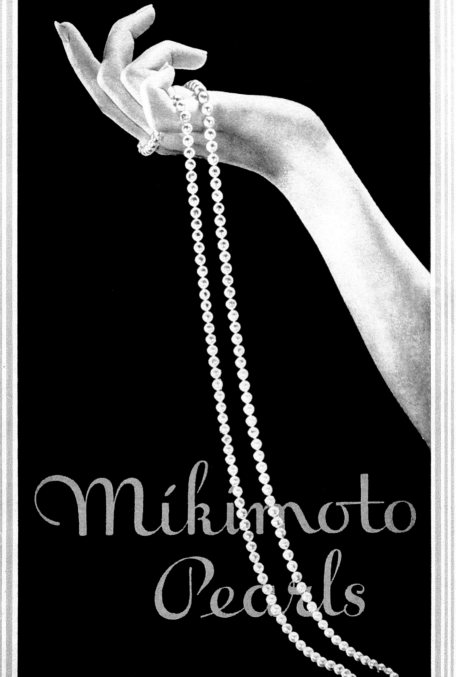

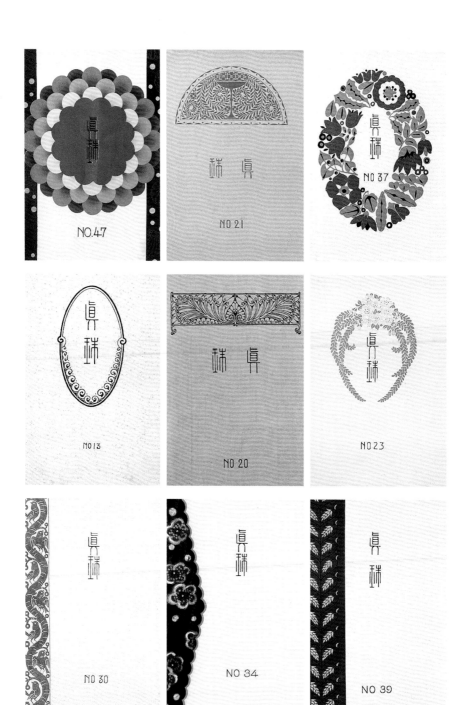

NO.47　NO 21　NO 37

NO 13　NO 20　NO 23

NO 30　NO 34　NO 39

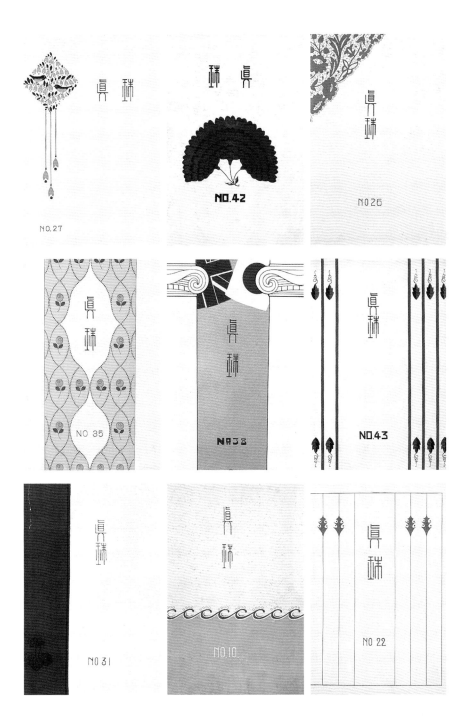

NO.27

NO.42

NO 26

NO 35

Nº 38

NO.43

NO 31

NO.10

NO 22

KRIEGHOFF

MIC IC
MIKIMOTO
DISCOVERER OF MAKING
THE METHOD PRODUCE
OYSTERS PEARLS

OYSTER WITH
ARTIFICIAL PEARL

PUTTING OFF IN THE BOAT

Susan Strasberg

These Mikimoto cultured pearls
(in their original oval leather and
velvet box) were given to
Marilyn Monroe on her honeymoon
with Joe DeMaggio in Japan.
Marilyn eventually gave them
to my mother, Paula, who was
her friend and drama coach on
"Bustop", "Prince and the Showgirl,"
"Misfits", "Some Like It Hot", etc.,
as a Christmas present. I wrote
about these pearls in my two
"memoirs "Bittersweet" and recently
"Marilyn and Me." After Marilyn's
death my mother wanted me
to have them and gave them to me.
The pearls were one of the very
few pieces of quality jewelery
Marilyn ever owned — everything
else was costume. There are numerous
photos of M.M. in her pearls.
Susan Strasberg
June 29, 1998

MIKIMOTO PEARLS

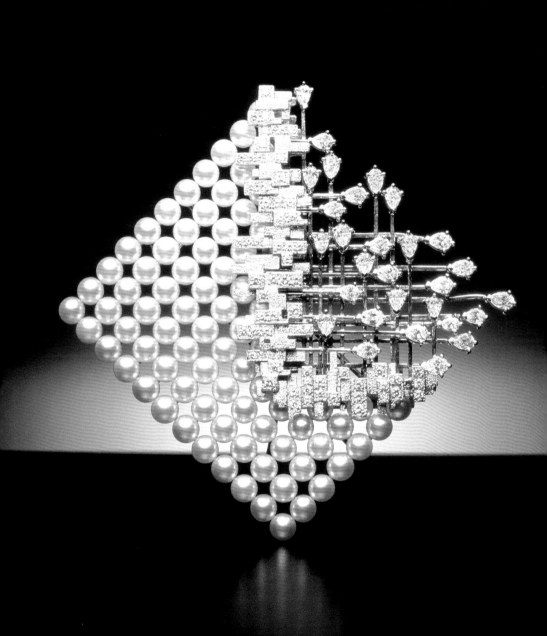

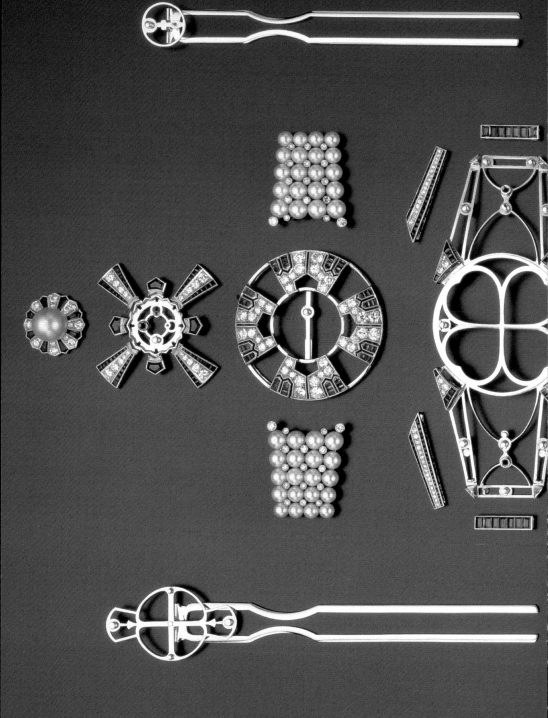

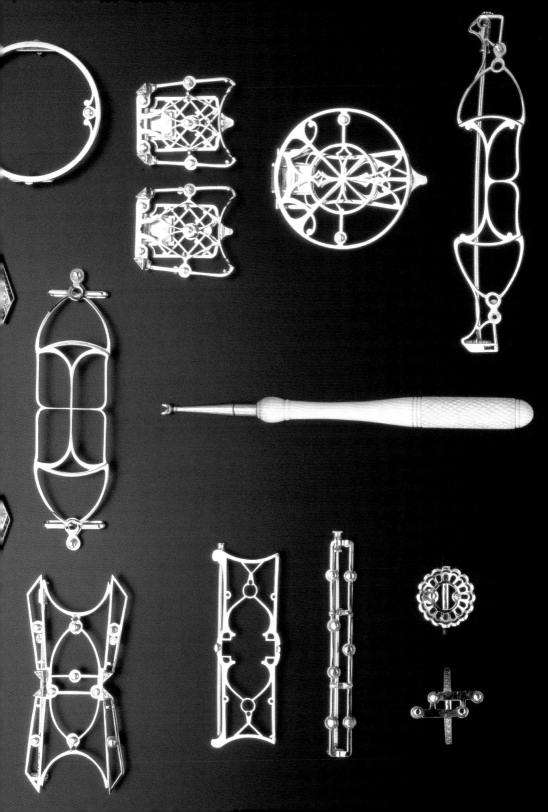

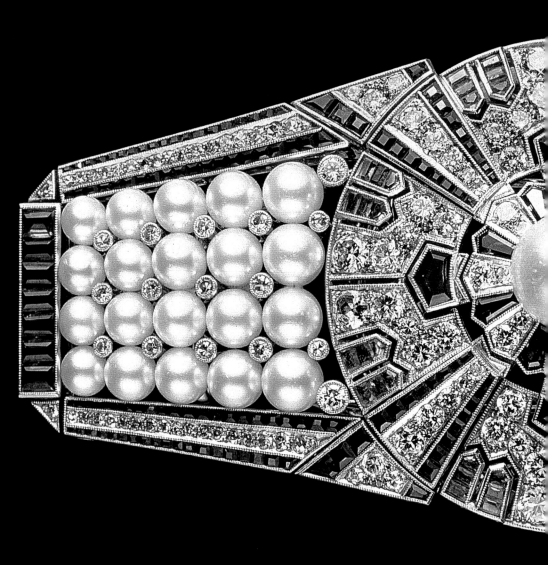

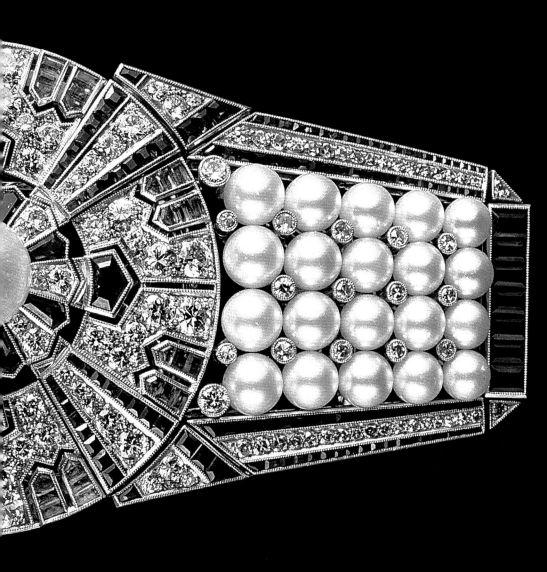

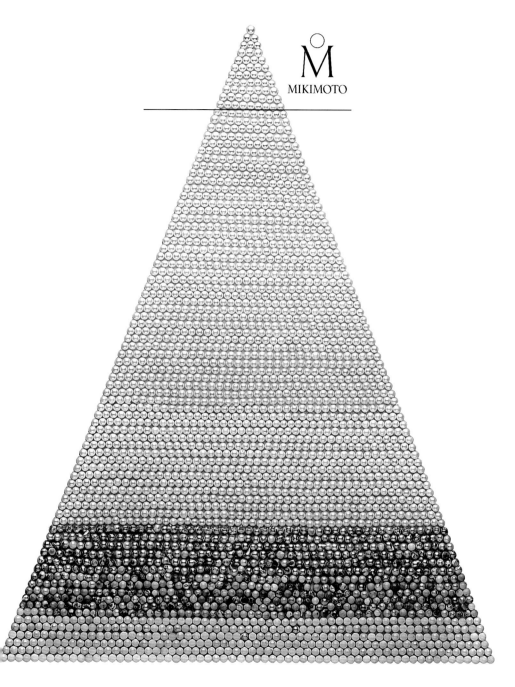

MIKIMOTO in Relation to Japan's Harvest of Akoya Cultured Pearls

Chronology

1893: Kokichi Mikimoto cultures the world's first semi-spherical pearl, ultimately harvesting five Akoya pearls on July 11. These are the first pearls ever grown by man.

1899: The first Mikimoto Pearl Store opens in Tokyo's Ginza district.

1905: Kokichi Mikimoto succeeds in culturing spherical pearls.

1907: Japan's first full-scale jewelry production facility opens, the Mikimoto Gold Work Factory.

1913: The first Mikimoto Pearl Store opens in London, followed by establishments in Shanghai, Bombay, New York, Los Angeles, and Chicago.

1914: Mikimoto establishes the world's first Black South Sea pearl farm on Ishigaki Island in Okinawa, Japan. Black lipped pearl cultivation begins on the beaches of Misakihama and Kannonzaki, Nakura Bay, and Ishigaki Island in Okinawa.

1922: Mikimoto researchers culture silver-lipped pearls on the South Pacific island of Palau.

1926: The pearl-encrusted Five-Storied Pagoda creates a sensation at the Philadelphia World's Fair. This model of the five-tiered pagoda at Horyuji Temple in Japan is now on display at Mikimoto Pearl Island.

1927: Kokichi Mikimoto meets Thomas Edison at Edison's home in New York. Edison, an avid Mikimoto jewelry collector, told the company founder that "there are two things which couldn't be made at my laboratory—diamonds and pearls."

1929: The first Mikimoto store opens in Paris under the sign "Nikimoto." The misprint is corrected years later.

1931: Craftsmen harvest a ten-millimeter pearl on Ishigaki Island, Okinawa.

1932: In a gesture that emphasizes the importance of quality, Kokichi Mikimoto burns 720,000 poor quality pearls in front of the Kobe Chamber of Commerce in Japan. Foreign journalists report on this event around the world.

1933: Mikimoto artisans create a 1/60th scale model of the Mount Vernon estate, residence of the first United States president, George Washington. The model, exhibited at the Chicago World's Fair, is donated to the Smithsonian Institute, where it still stands on display.

1937: The *Yagurama* (Wheels of Arrows), a sash clip with twelve interchangeable settings, attracts attention at the Paris Expo. It is sold in Paris to a private collector and reappears at auction in New York fifty-two years later. The Mikimoto Pearl Island company buys the piece, where it is now on display.

1939: Artisans create a model of the Liberty Bell for the New York World's Fair, expressing hope in that troubled time. The Mikimoto Liberty Bell now resides at Mikimoto Pearl Island.

1957: The Mikimoto company donates a pearl crown to the National Cherry Blossom Festival in Washington, D.C., a celebration of Japanese-American ties.

1969: The brooch Prelude to Space, designed by Yuji Takahashi and crafted by Kiyoshi Nishimura, wins the most prestigious award in jewelry design: the Diamonds-International Award from De Beers Diamonds.

1972: The company name changes to K. Mikimoto & Co., Ltd.

1974: The main store in Ginza boasts one of the largest jewelry sales floor areas in the world.

1975: The New York store opens on Fifth Avenue, Manhattan.

1990: The Mikimoto μ ("mu") Collection represents the essence of Japanese jewelry culture. Designed to represent the best of Mikimoto's experience and expertise in materials, design, and craftsmanship, each piece is numbered, and the design drawings are permanently stored.

1995: Mikimoto opens a store on New Bond Street in London.

2001: Mikimoto creates one-of-a kind pieces with New York fashion designers Badgely Mischka, Oscar de la Renta, Carolina Herrera, and Vera Wang that sold at auction for charity.

2002: Mikimoto creates the official Miss Universe crown. The tiara-style crown features a phoenix-wing motif as a symbol of eternal beauty.

2005: Mikimoto opens Ginza 2 in Tokyo. The architect, Toyo Ito, draws his inspiration from the mysteriousness of a jewelry box, imagining bubbles and petals floating around pearls. The building has become a Ginza landmark.

2008: Mikimoto celebrates the 150th anniversary of Kokichi Mikimoto's birth.

Mikimoto

Johannes Vermeer (van Delft) painted *Girl with the Pearl Earring* circa 1665. The painting now resides at Mauristhuis, The Hague, The Netherlands. © Scala/Art Resource, NY.

A large Black South Sea pearl harvested at Ishigaki Island, Okinawa. © Mikimoto.

An illustration from *100 poems by 100 poets* by Katsushika Hokusai shows female divers surrounding Sangi Takamura, a high-ranking civil servant from the ninth century who fell out of favor and was banished to far-away islands. © Erich Lessing/Art Resource, NY.

A view of Mikimoto pearl beds in Toba, Japan, 1986. © Robert Holmes/CORBIS.

Strands of pearls, circa 2000. © Macduff Everton/CORBIS.

Workers lift baskets of nucleated oysters onto a raft for the Mikimoto company in Toba Bay, circa 1947. © Horace Bristol/CORBIS.

A South Sea Pearl, diamond, tourmaline, and emerald brooch designed in 1983. © Mikimoto.

Oysters of various sizes. This image from *Pearls: A Natural History*. Photography by Craig Chesek, courtesy the Library, American Museum of Natural History.

Cover image for the 1983 catalog celebrating the 90th anniversary of the Exhibition of Cultured Pearl Innovation. © Mikimoto.

As president of the Japan Marine Pearl Association, Kokichi Mikimoto burned 720,000 inferior-quality pearls in 1932, reestablishing the reputation for quality within the pearl industry. © Mikimoto.

Model Christy Turlington in Jean Paul Gaultier and Mikimoto pearl earrings. Photo credit: Patrick Demarchelier/ *Vogue* © 1988 Condé Nast Publications, Inc.

In 1929, the Paris store opens at 7 Rue de Chateaud under a sign painted "Niki-moto." The misspelling was later corrected. © Mikimoto.

A **woman** strings cultured pearls at the Mikimoto factory in Toba, Japan, circa 1947. © Horace Bristol/CORBIS.
Mikimoto's catalog advertisement for the Chicago World Expo, 1933. © Mikimoto.

This **sash clip** was reissued in 1934, based on a design in *Pearl* catalog No. 54. Nineteen pearls and 2.14 carats of diamonds are set in platinum. © MIKIMOTO PEARL ISLAND CO., LTD.

A **selection** of eighteen catalog covers. Mikimoto published *Pearl* catalogs from 1908–1938, issued by number. © Mikimoto.

The New York Herald Tribune featured Kokichi and the Mikimoto company in its October 9, 1904, edition. Photo circa 1907. © Mikimoto.
Archival photo of the Mikimoto store decorated for the Christmas holiday in the Ginza district of Tokyo, circa 1907. © Mikimoto.

An **18 karat gold** Akoya pearl, ruby, and diamond necklace with matching 18 karat gold ruby and diamond ring. Designed in 1986. © Mikimoto.
The Cherry Blossom Crown was donated to the annual Cherry Blossom Festival in Washington, D.C., in 1957. The 18 karat gold crown features 1,600 Akoya pearls. © Mikimoto.

In 1954, Joe DiMaggio gave Marilyn Monroe, his bride, this 16-inch strand of 44 Akoya pearls during their honeymoon in Japan, here shown in their original oval box. © NIWA Photography.

Mikimoto purchased Marilyn Monroe's original necklace from the actress Susan Strasberg. Strasberg had received the pearls from her mother, Paula Strasberg, a friend of Monroe's. © Mikimoto (America) Co., Ltd.

Marilyn Monroe waves for the cameras wearing her Mikimoto pearls in Santa Monica, Calif., on October 27, 1954. © Bettmann/CORBIS.zz

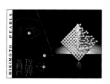

The invitation and announcement of the new, three-story Mikimoto store opened in the Ginza district of Tokyo in 1953. © Mikimoto.

This 18 karat gold brooch with Akoya pearls and diamonds won the De Beers Diamonds-International Award in 1969. © Mikimoto.

This design sketch of an Akoya pearl, diamond, and platinum headpiece, circa 1915 was inspired by European styles of the time. © Mikimoto.

Designed for the Miss Universe pageant in 2002, this crown of about 800 diamonds—almost 18 carats—and about 120 South Sea and Akoya pearls ranging in size from 3–18 mm., is valued at $250,000. The design evokes the image of a rising phoenix, representing status, power, and beauty. © SAEED KHAN/AFP/Getty Images.

Black South Sea cultured pearls in varying shades with Mikimoto signature clasps Campaign 2006-2007. © 2005 Claus Wickrath.

Grace Kelly wears Mikimoto pearls in her publicity stills for the film *Rear Window* (1954). © Underwood & Underwood/CORBIS.

An Akoya pearl, diamond, and 18 karat white gold sash clip with a grapevine design. © MIKIMOTO PEARL ISLAND CO., LTD.

An archival photo of Kokichi Mikimoto measuring pearls, circa 1951. © Mikimoto.

The multifunctional *Yagurama* (Wheels of Arrows), shown here deconstructed, can be joined together in 12 different ways to attached bases. It was first exhibited at the World Exposition in Paris, 1937. © MIKIMOTO PEARL ISLAND CO., LTD.

The *Yagurama* (Wheels of Arrows), shown here as a sash clip, features one 8.75 mm. pearl at its center and twenty pearls of 3.5–4.5 mm. on each side. Diamonds and caliber-cut sapphires are set in its platinum base. © MIKIMOTO PEARL ISLAND CO., LTD.

Detail of two South Sea pearl necklaces with the Mikimoto 18 karat yellow gold clasp and logo charm, 2005. © Chip Forelli.
Model Christy Turlington wears a Mikimoto earring to complement the "RICH" t-shirt by Tracey Glick for Boy-Girl Tees underneath a sequined jacket. Photo credit: Patrick Demarchelier/*Vogue* © 1988 Condé Nast Publications, Inc.

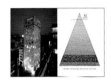

View of the Mikimoto Ginza 2 building designed by the architect Toyo Ito. Ginza district, Tokyo. © Mikimoto.
The Mikimoto Pearl Pyramid shows how few pearls make the coveted Mikimoto grade. © Mikimoto (America) Co., Ltd.

The Mikimoto Milano collection ring by Giovanna Broggian in 18 karat yellow gold, 2005. © Chip Forelli.
Model Jacquetta Wheeler wears a triple-strand pearl necklace by Mikimoto and a white eyelet bustier-top cocktail dress by Oscar de la Renta. Photo credit: Arthur Elgort/*Vogue* © 2002 Condé Nast Publications, Inc.

The many colors of Mikimoto pearls. © Nana Watanabe.

Notes

[1] Joyce, Kristin and Shellei Addison. *Pearls: Ornament and Obsession* (New York: Prentice Hall, 1992), 35.

[2] Quoted in *Pearls: Ornament and Obsession* (New York: Prentice Hall, 1992), 45.

[3] Pliny. *Natural History.*

[4] Eunson, Robert. *The Pearl King* (North Clarenden, VT: Tuttle Publishing, 1964), 12.

[5] Ibid., 72.

[6] Ibid., 73.

[7] Ibid., 74.

[8] Kokichi Mikimoto Memorial Hall, 12.

[9] Eunson, Robert. *The Pearl King* (North Clarenden, VT: Tuttle Publishing, 1964), 120.

[10] Ibid., 134.

[11] Article in *The New York Herald*, October 9, 1904, quoted in *The Pearl King*, Robert Eunson (North Clarenden, VT: Tuttle Publishing, 1964), 145.

Acknowledgments

The publisher wishes to thank: Kyojiro Hata, Tom Baione at The American Museum of Natural History; Jennifer Belt at Art Resource; Rebecca Behan; Dan Brennan; Marissa Caputo at IMG; Luc Alexis Chasleries; Craig Chesek; Alyson Dusseault; Julian Fifer and Nana Watanabe; Chip Forelli; Claire Fortune and Dawn Lucas at The Condé Nast Publications, Inc.; Andrea Moretti at NIWA Photography; Laziz Hamani; Erika Imberti; Lisa Jacobson and Lauren Meisels at United Talent Agency; Dilcia Johnson and Norman Currie at Corbis; Nina Schroeren; Christy Turlington; Larry Van Cassele, Marcia Dover Hoffman, and Wilfred Tenaillon at Getty Images; Jacquetta Wheeler; and Claus Wickrath.